ANIMAL BATTLES

BLACK BEAR VS. MOUNTAIN LION

BY NATHAN SOMMER

BELLWETHER MEDIA • MINNEAPOLIS, MN

Torque brims with excitement perfect for thrill-seekers of all kinds. Discover daring survival skills, explore uncharted worlds, and marvel at mighty engines and extreme sports. In *Torque* books, anything can happen. Are you ready?

This edition first published in 2025 by Bellwether Media, Inc.

No part of this publication may be reproduced in whole or in part without written permission of the publisher.
For information regarding permission, write to Bellwether Media, Inc., Attention: Permissions Department,
6012 Blue Circle Drive, Minnetonka, MN 55343.

Library of Congress Cataloging-in-Publication Data

LC record for Black Bear vs. Mountain Lion available at:
https://lccn.loc.gov/2024036209

Text copyright © 2025 by Bellwether Media, Inc. TORQUE and associated logos are trademarks and/or registered trademarks of Bellwether Media, Inc.

Editor: Suzane Nguyen   Designer: Hunter Demmin

Printed in the United States of America, North Mankato, MN.

TABLE OF CONTENTS

THE COMPETITORS	4
SECRET WEAPONS	10
ATTACK MOVES	16
READY, FIGHT!	20
GLOSSARY	22
TO LEARN MORE	23
INDEX	24

THE COMPETITORS

North America's forests are home to many **predators**. Black bears are some of the largest among them. These **opportunistic** hunters eat whatever they can get their paws on.

Black bears share some **habitats** with mountain lions. These **apex predators** can leap on and defeat much larger **prey**. Which predator is more deadly?

Black bears are **mammals**. They have short tails, rounded ears, and stocky bodies. They grow up to 6 feet (1.8 meters) long. They can weigh over 600 pounds (272 kilograms).

Black bears are the most common bears in North America. They are found in forests and mountains. In the winter, the bears build dens in trees or underground.

BLACK BEAR PROFILE

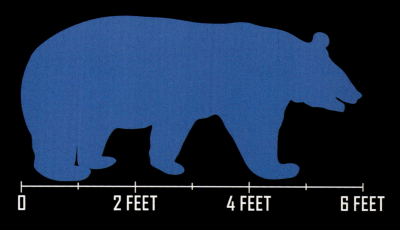

0   2 FEET   4 FEET   6 FEET

LENGTH
UP TO 6 FEET
(1.8 METERS)

WEIGHT
OVER 600 POUNDS
(272 KILOGRAMS)

HABITATS

FORESTS

MOUNTAINS

SWAMPS

BLACK BEAR RANGE

■ RANGE

MOUNTAIN LION PROFILE

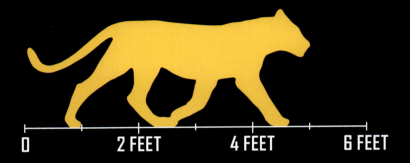

0   2 FEET   4 FEET   6 FEET

LENGTH
UP TO 5 FEET
(1.5 METERS)

WEIGHT
UP TO 158 POUNDS
(72 KILOGRAMS)

HABITATS

SWAMPS

DESERTS

MOUNTAINS

FORESTS

MOUNTAIN LION RANGE

RANGE

Mountain lions are large wild cats. These mammals weigh up to 158 pounds (72 kilograms). They grow up to 5 feet (1.5 meters) long from head to tail. The cats have beige fur, long tails, and strong back legs.

Mountain lions live throughout South America and western North America. The **solitary** predators make homes where they can find food.

WIDESPREAD WILD CATS

Mountain lions have the largest home range of any wild cat in the Americas.

SECRET WEAPONS

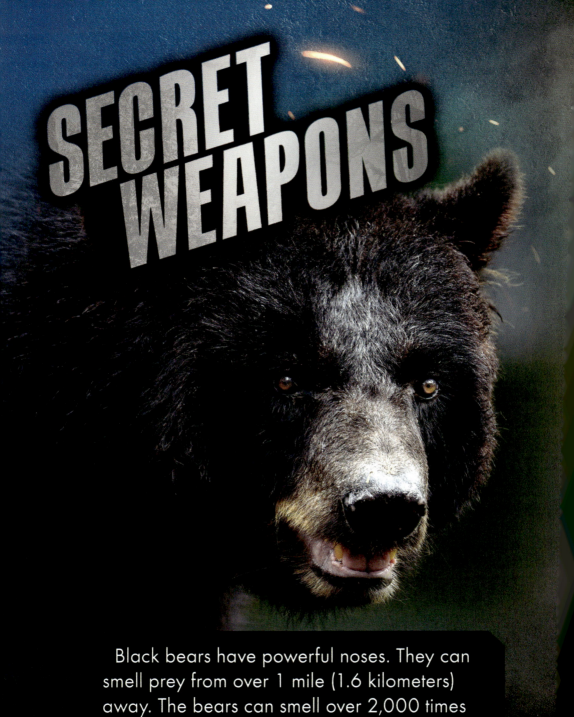

Black bears have powerful noses. They can smell prey from over 1 mile (1.6 kilometers) away. The bears can smell over 2,000 times better than a human!

Large eyes with special **retinas** give mountain lions excellent night vision. The cats spot objects in the dark that most animals cannot see. This helps them hunt at night!

SECRET WEAPONS

BLACK BEAR

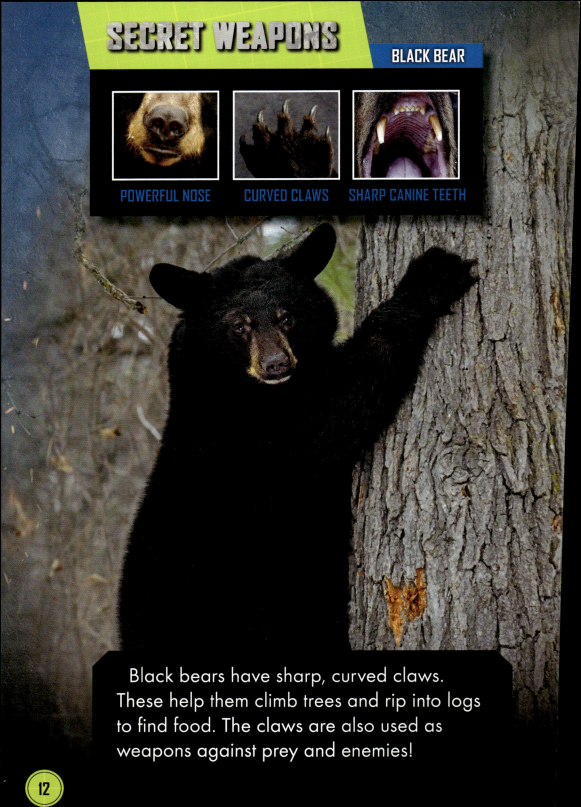

POWERFUL NOSE — **CURVED CLAWS** — **SHARP CANINE TEETH**

Black bears have sharp, curved claws. These help them climb trees and rip into logs to find food. The claws are also used as weapons against prey and enemies!

LEAPING DISTANCE

MOUNTAIN LION: 40 FEET (12 METERS)

0 — 10 FEET — 20 FEET — 30 FEET — 40 FEET — 50 FEET

SCHOOL BUS: 45 FEET (13 METERS)

0 — 10 FEET — 20 FEET — 30 FEET — 40 FEET — 50 FEET

Strong back legs help mountain lions leap far. The cats can leap up to 40 feet (12 meters) in one jump! Most prey cannot escape their leaps.

Black bears have 42 teeth. They use their sharp **canine teeth** to hurt enemies and **grip** small prey. Their teeth also help them pull apart **carrion**.

BLACK BEAR CANINE TOOTH SIZE

3 INCHES
(7.6 CENTIMETERS)

TOP-NOTCH TONGUES

Black bears have long, powerful tongues. They use these to lick up bugs to eat!

SECRET WEAPONS

MOUNTAIN LION

NIGHT VISION

STRONG BACK LEGS

POWERFUL JAWS

Mountain lions have powerful jaws. They use these to sink their sharp teeth into prey. The cats can crush bones with one forceful bite!

ATTACK MOVES

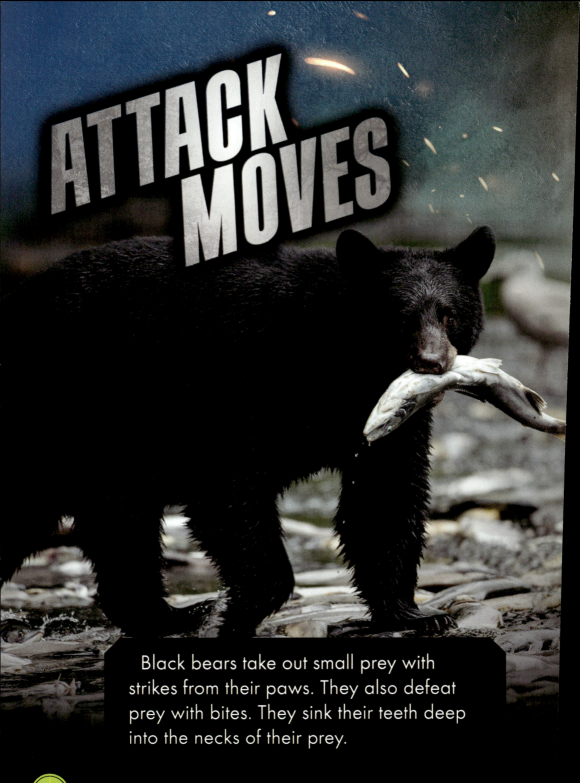

Black bears take out small prey with strikes from their paws. They also defeat prey with bites. They sink their teeth deep into the necks of their prey.

Mountain lions **ambush** their prey. They **stalk** their meals from behind. Sometimes they lie in wait for prey to pass by. Then the cats attack at the perfect moment!

MAJOR APPETITES

Mountain lions can eat up to 30 pounds (13.6 kilograms) of meat in one sitting!

Black bears use speed to chase larger prey. They defeat it with strikes from their sharp claws. The bears will eat large carrion for days if they cannot find food.

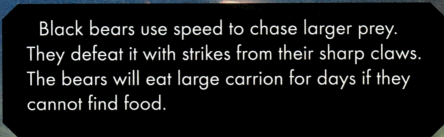

SUPER SPRINTERS

Black bears can run up to 30 miles (48 kilometers) per hour while chasing prey.

Mountain lions leap on prey from behind. Then they defeat it with bites to the neck. The cats often hide large meals under leaves or sticks.

READY, FIGHT!

A black bear approaches carrion. Suddenly, a mountain lion leaps on the bear. The cat fights to protect its food! It bites the bear.

The bear bites the lion. It strikes the cat hard with its large paws. The injured mountain lion runs away. The black bear has stolen a meal today!

GLOSSARY

ambush—to carry out a surprise attack

apex predators—animals at the top of the food chain that are not preyed upon by other animals

canine teeth—long, pointed teeth that are often the sharpest in the mouth

carrion—the remains of a dead animal

grip—to hold tight

habitats—the homes or areas where animals prefer to live

mammals—warm-blooded animals that have backbones and feed their young milk

opportunistic—taking advantage of a situation

predators—animals that hunt other animals for food

prey—animals that are hunted by other animals for food

retinas—the back parts of the eye that take in light and help the brain understand what it is seeing

solitary—related to living alone

stalk—to follow closely and quietly

TO LEARN MORE

AT THE LIBRARY

Klepinger, Teresa. *Cougar vs. Wolf.* Minneapolis, Minn.: Kaleidoscope, 2022.

Sommer, Nathan. *Burmese Python vs. Sun Bear.* Minneapolis, Minn.: Bellwether Media, 2024.

Winter, Steve, and Sharon Guynup. *The Ultimate Book of Big Cats.* Washington, D.C.: National Geographic Kids, 2022.

ON THE WEB

Factsurfer.com gives you a safe, fun way to find more information.

1. Go to www.factsurfer.com

2. Enter "black bear vs. mountain lion" into the search box and click 🔍.

3. Select your book cover to see a list of related content.

INDEX

ambush, 17
attack, 17
bite, 15, 16, 19, 20
canine teeth, 14
carrion, 14, 18, 20
claws, 12, 18
climb, 12
color, 9
dens, 6
enemies, 12, 14
eyes, 11
food, 9, 12, 17, 18, 19, 20
habitats, 4, 5, 6, 7, 8
hunters, 4, 11
jaws, 15
leap, 5, 13, 19, 20
legs, 9, 13
mammals, 6, 9
night, 11

North America, 4, 6, 9
noses, 10
paws, 4, 16, 20
predators, 4, 5, 9
prey, 5, 10, 12, 13, 14, 15, 16, 17, 18, 19
range, 4, 6, 7, 8, 9
size, 4, 6, 7, 8, 9, 14
solitary, 9
South America, 9
speed, 18
stalk, 17
teeth, 14, 15, 16
tongues, 14
weapons, 12, 15

The images in this book are reproduced through the courtesy of: Steve Boer, front cover (black bear); Nolte Lourens, front cover (mountain lion); BGSmith, p. 4; sirtravelalot, p. 5; Christopher MacDonald, pp. 6-7; Warren Metcalf, pp. 8-9, 13, 15 (strong back legs); DSlight_photography, p. 10; Kwadrat, p. 11; Holly Kuchera, p. 12; jadimages, p. 12 (powerful nose); Berke, p. 12 (curved claws); Jim Cumming, p. 12 (sharp canine teeth); GreenReynolds/ Getty, p. 14; JohnPitcher/ Getty, p. 15; Evgeniyqw, p. 15 (night vision); SteffenTravel, p. 15 (powerful jaws); Alexandre Boudet, p. 16; TigerStocks, p. 17; Jean Landry, p. 18; Design Pics/ Alamy, p. 19; Marques, pp. 20-21 (mountain lion); Tammi Mild/ Getty, pp. 20-21.